Theory Paper   Grade 1   2017   A
Model Answers

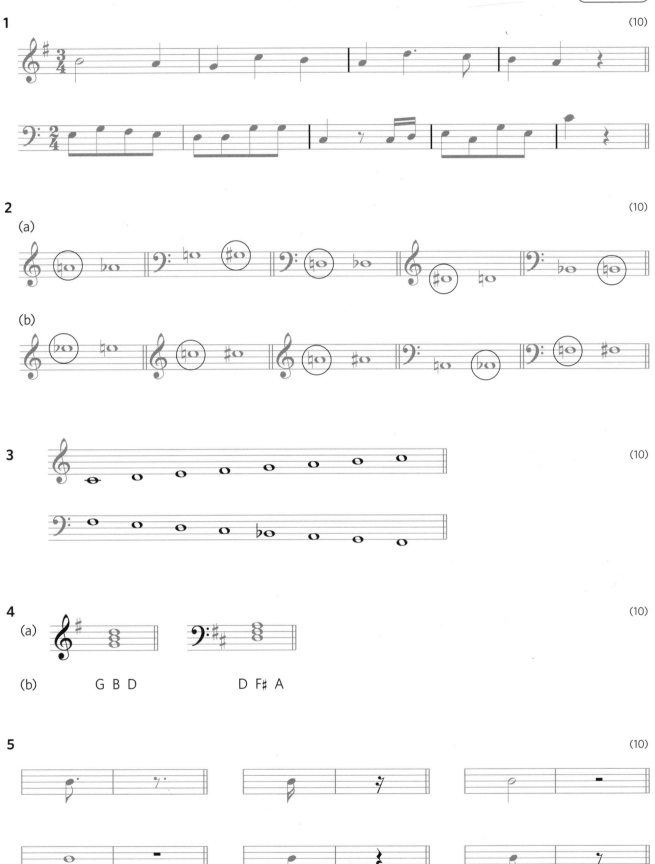

6   6th   2nd   4th   (10)

    8th / 8ve   5th   7th

7   (10)

(a) 5th   4th   2nd   3rd   7th   6th   8th   5th   1st

                                                   8ve / 1st   8th / 8ve

(b) E

8   (10)

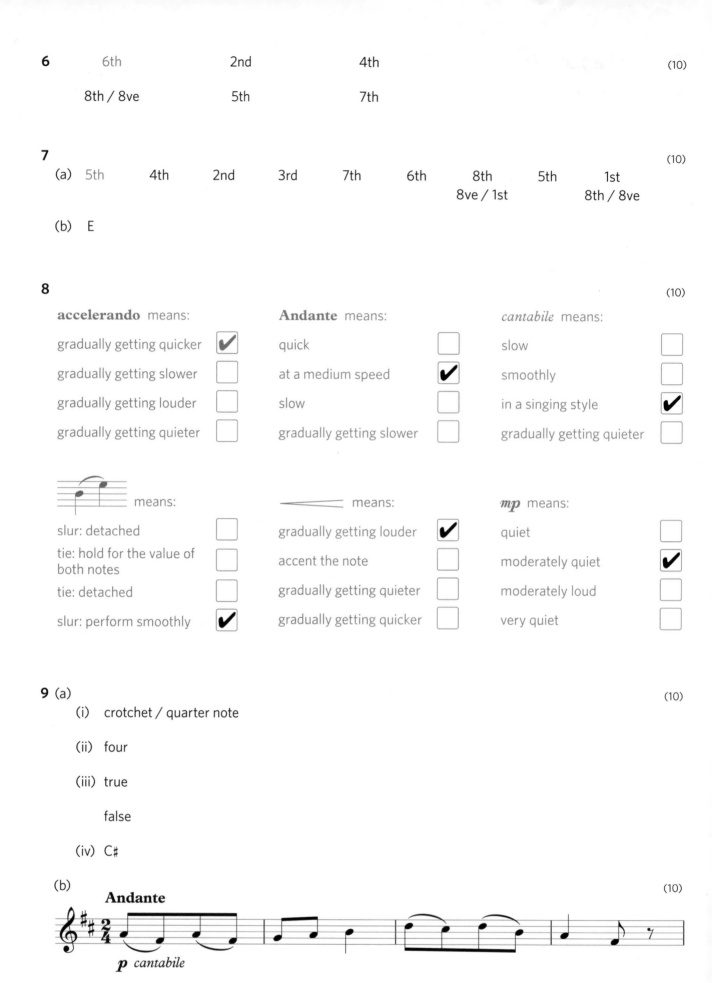

9 (a)   (10)

    (i)   crotchet / quarter note

    (ii) four

    (iii) true

           false

    (iv) C♯

(b)   (10)

Theory Paper   Grade 1   2017   B
Model Answers

1 (10)

(a)

(b)

2   *pp*   *p*   *mp*   *mf*   *f*   *ff*   (10)

3 (10)

(a)

(b)

4 (10)

5 (10)

(a) G   A   C   F#   E   G   G   B   D

(b) crotchet / quarter note

6 (10)

G major   F major   D major

C major   D major   G major

7 (10)

8 (10)

Lento means:

smoothly ☐

gradually getting slower ☐

at a medium speed ☐

slow ☑

Allegretto means:

slow ☐

fairly quick ☑

gradually getting quicker ☐

gradually getting slower ☐

p means:

quiet ☑

very quiet ☐

moderately quiet ☐

moderately loud ☐

cresc. means:

gradually getting slower ☐

gradually getting quicker ☐

gradually getting louder ☑

gradually getting quieter ☐

accelerando means:

accent the note ☐

fairly quick ☐

gradually getting louder ☐

gradually getting quicker ☑

> means:

staccato: detached ☐

accent the note ☑

gradually getting quieter ☐

legato: smoothly ☐

9 (a) (10)

(i)   two

(ii) 5

(iii) 3rd

(iv) true

(v)   four

(b) (10)

Theory Paper Grade 1 2017 C
Model Answers

1 (10)

(a)

(b)

2 F major   G major   C major (10)

D major   C major   G major

3 (10)

4 (10)

5 Key C major (10)

Key G major

Key D major

6 (10)

(a) 7th   3rd   8th /   6th   7th   5th   1st /   4th   2nd

                             8ve / 1st   8th / 8ve

(b) C♯

7 (10)

8 (10)

a tempo means:		$\quad$ = 48 means:		*cantabile* means:	
held back	☐	48 crotchet beats	☐	at a medium speed	☐
in time	✔	48 crotchet notes	☐	slow	☐
the end	☐	48 crotchet beats in a minute	✔	repeat from the beginning	☐
a little	☐	48 crotchets in the melody	☐	in a singing style	✔

Adagio means:		means:		means:	
slow	✔	tie: hold for the value of both notes	☐	gradually getting quicker	☐
held back	☐	slur: detached	☐	gradually getting quieter	✔
gradually getting slower	☐	tie: detached	☐	gradually getting louder	☐
fairly quick	☐	slur: perform smoothly	✔	gradually getting slower	☐

9 (a) (10)

   (i)   minim / half note

   (ii) Bar 1 / 2 / 4 / 5

   (iii) true

        false

   (iv) A

(b) (10)

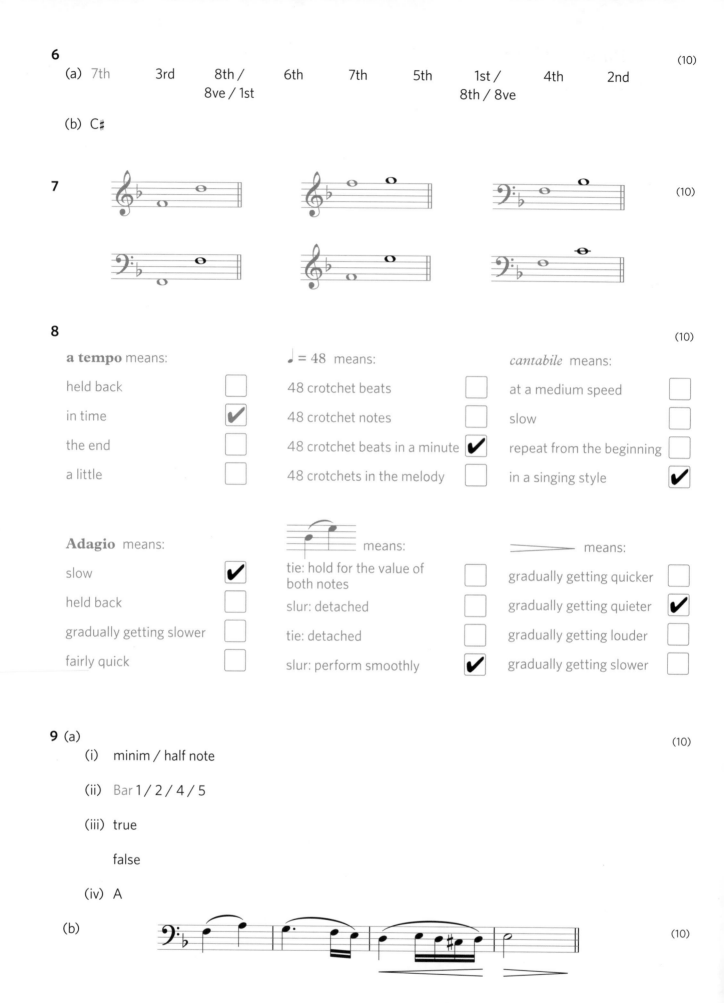

Theory Paper   Grade 1   2017   S
Model Answers

1   (10)

2   *ff*   *f*   *mf*   *mp*   *p*   *pp*   (10)

3 G major   D major   F major   (10)

F major   C major   G major

4   (10)

(a) G   F   D   A   C   E   G   B   C

(b) semiquaver / 16th note

5   (10)

6   (10)

7 6th 5th 7th (10)

4th 2nd 8th / 8ve

8 (10)

8va̅ ̅ ̅ ̅ ̅ ̅ ̅ ̅ ̅ ̅ ̅ ̅ ̅ ̅⌐ means:

perform the notes smoothly ☐
perform an octave lower ☐
pause on the note or rest ☐
perform an octave higher ☑

Allegro means:

fairly quick ☐
quick ☑
at a medium speed ☐
slow ☐

ritardando (rit.) means:

gradually getting slower ☑
gradually getting quieter ☐
slow ☐
gradually getting louder ☐

f means:

very loud ☐
loud ☑
gradually getting louder ☐
moderately loud ☐

means:

slur: perform smoothly ☐
tie: detached ☐
slur: detached ☐
tie: hold for the value of both notes ☑

means:

staccato: detached ☐
legato: smoothly ☐
accent the note ☑
gradually getting quieter ☐

9 (a) (10)

(i) two

(ii) eight

(iii) *legato* (smoothly)

(iv) 5th

(v) Bar 2 / 4 / 5

(b) (10)

Allegro moderato

f

10